Low Commotion

Richard MacNeill

"Low Commotion"
Copyright by Richard MacNeill
Cover art by Marco Melgrati

www.BuaidhArts.com

The Role art
 inspires

dedication

※

I don't have the answers
reality is what we change
reality is what we accept

※

Adherents to government
complain about systems
until the systems work for them.
I have no allowance to governing agendas.
I do not need to pledge allegiance.
Anyone ordering a pledge of allegiance
is clearly unsure of themselves,
afraid of not being.
Culture killers
relay rhetoric to the unknowing.
Anything requiring uniformity is a trap, a lie,
a trick to make your mind obey.
It is not pride;
it is conformity
and pride in conformity.
A good man needs no attire
to make his world go round.
A good man sees it is not
what makes the world go round; it is we.
They are not upholders of the law.
They are upholders of anarchy,
inane protectors of their worthy cause
and filled to the brim with insight toward flaws
in another man, yet not you,
not you,
who reap so easily the felled tree withers
and set the right path upon a fallen dream of…

Where, in all these lands, are the righteous
who call themselves merry?

Mechanical drones
claim everything they do is for freedom,
however out of context and heinous.
Humans have the freedom
to act in a herd.
Art is true freedom.
Find your choices.

We see the moonrise before it is risen.

We can applaud good parents.
Parents embrace parts of themselves
no one knew existed.
Children live with
the darkest parts
of their parents
and feel every untaught emotion.

Do you teach a soul to writhe in fire?
Where do we go wandering around the vacancies?
Where do we go discovering the fullness?

She said, You will not be there when we need you.
So, I did not do what did not feel right.
I cast away the casting away
when she said, You will hurt us all.
and returned to make this right.
What I thought were good choices
were easy rebellion and seeing
such choices can be made
not because they are right,
but because they are easy.
Do not go forth into what is not your crime.
I decided to cultivate the right mind.

※

Everywhere brings out what is in us.
We ignite what is within all.
The only time I've hurt myself is when I was angry.
Every time I bet on myself, I win.
Madness has its rewards.

※

Carbonated copies
of navels swimming in anticipation
with warriors' declarations,
wordless and primal.
Where were these Hermes's accolades
when children laughed and ran and played
before the dreadful merchant told them
what they must do?

※

Howling to you, my brother.
Break me from this cage.
No one has ever done for me
what I would not do myself.
I sit silently
devouring the cage.
Its bones shall become my bones.
When they come to feed me,
I shall escape.

A writer's life is silent constant explosions.

※

My standards are high and cruel
The frilly, tall palm tree
The Hector's view wide believing eucalyptus
 the hero
mistaken sadness
caring courses
mistaken madness
regretting mistaken
giving symphonies
The western sun
alights our trails
the moon is pregnant
reaching out toward the sun

Thanksgiving sans thought…

These liberals… Obama… The Clintons are gonna keep makin' money… 'cause the economy… Look at Putin… Did someone throw a plastic bag in the fire? Good thing there aren't any environmentalists out here. Oooh, the fumes. Geez… Fucking nigger. It all starts there. Like when something's wrong with the computer, it all starts at the motherboard.

Rushing to have everything. We see, you have life.

※

Do not be fooled by yourself, anymore. You are not
under sway of your thoughts. Your thoughts
are beholden to you.

Holding a balloon doesn't chain you.
Seeing chains chains you.

Are we free to love?
Do we love?
God says, 'it's nothing.'
God says, 'We'll see.'

Fear is a cult.

※

We are born to make fire
and keep fire going
and teach the fire and the wave-riding.

※

'Laws' are words constantly changing. Why do you hold the
law as anything other than a transient whim? Law is nothing.

※

And the hundredth time I said there are no rules.
And I became sick. Sick of my own heart.
Sick of what I allowed my heart to do.
Or what my heart allowed me to do.
I'm not sure.
A hundred years live in one moment
where the cool wet night splashes calm
and rain cascades into our tent
as we force the revival of mystery.
I'm not sure.
A hundred thousand years wail open a mind
ready to take all at the forfeit of wrong.
The black ants swarm our childhood memories
and we accept a rather higher view of ourselves than
we deserve.
I'm not sure.
Where, oh where do our buffalo roam
managed not to exeunt the worldstage
and autumn cringes at the wailing streetcage
as the fierce hungry ages knock ready to feast upon the
jailors and bring spring?
I'm not sure.
One question in a thousand will get a needy answer.
The rest is a smile and an ask where you will.
How many times you are never apart
till you roll in the dirt and the ocean of your heart.
I'm not sure.

※

We judge ourselves too harshly.
There is a world, the world, in which our conceptions are
not ruled and not the rule. We are free.

※

When you find the ring of true love,
nothing changes. The wearer of the ring is unfathomable
and must discover one's self.

※

Be careful of being flattered;
   You feel good and go
     do something stupid.
   We don't always recognize a rare warm day
until someone points out the occupation
 and the slipping through symmetry
   you have done.
Oh, lucky days
 be worth the treasure
   I am calling from you.

And we are the shadow of a hand moving the glass door

※

Felt like living like a cat today.
Until I felt like getting up.
My kids share this occasional wish.
Lay around.
Lay in the shade.
Lay in the warm sun.
Get up to eat and lay around.
Find a secret spot.
Go to unload your bowels.
Explore everywhere you can climb
and escape outside to explore.
With the uncertainty of when you'll be able to come back in,
but knowing they love you, time takes its leisure.
Sometimes, those who love are cruel. They may, because
they love you and respect your right to nature, refuse to cut
you open and take your procreation. The effect, they keep
you outside once you start to spray and stink.
The children won't, but the adults put you into the world or
cut your maturity. Cruel trade.
The way. You die a death and live a life.

※

Work is published when it is read.
It will not be long
   and then you'll be an adult maestro.

※

I'll give you my sails.
And when you have children
   you can give them your sails
and they can learn from you
   the sails are your heart.
An Innis Àigh
   our souls continue.
I am happy for the pain which
   I can take for you.
A wolf doesn't need saving
   from being a wolf.
We live this wild life
   in Nature's trust.

※

Beach sand
more sea than land
the sign of a happy day
happy children
caring love
time will never take away

※

The zoo is loud

The silver kettle boils on the stove.
Near the top I watch,
  anticipating.
Hissing,
  three plumes of steam announce.
I returned from the cold breeze
  with no news.
Shapeless questions grasp at straws
  and I returned to continue wondering.
My eyes try not to see the nostalgia
  passing the schools of adolescent days.
My mind tries to see
  the dream-come-true when it hasn't.
Employees. Drown your sorrows
  knowing you are not hungry.
The spiritual hunger does not end.
No good comes from worry.
Feast on your pale demise.

※

Time is none of my business.
You find a string
which could've been something useful.
It's a memory, most useful of all.
Memory.

※

What are you going to do? Run away?
Something appears like it might kill you.
What are you going to do? Run away?
A man might go with no thought of thinking.
A fool, a beautiful romantic, might say to himself,
"I'll throw books at their heads."
and be on his way. Going.

Romans in their colosseum had gladiators.
The gladiators fought and died gruesome bloody deaths.
The poets stood outside, gazing up at the walls,
wondering.
Where does truth hide while gorging on bloody truth?
What is wrong? What is right? Is it a feeling?
Yes. Can we escape?
No. Yes, we are free fools.

※

I knew my true calling.
When I discovered my true calling, all was obvious.
When I discovered how obsolete it would be
in the public, I continued.
No one, save rock and roll gods, can claim
to have had their attitudes adjusted malignantly.
The truth, their attitudes are not what you see.
What society reveals to itself is only what it
shits and gawks at.
What we find when we seek, this is the only serene
reflection
of who we really are. This answer is unique
for each person.
Yet, society collects as trinkets the meaningless

and popularly obscure.
What truth? We sitcom lovers are the generations
of needing.
This is not to say everything is shit.
This is only to say shit rolls fast.
Comedy can change. Defensiveness can change.
And truth?
Truth is the underneath, the floor of the sea
which doesn't give a damn what you laugh at.
The comedy is there for us all.
The rage, the rage is most comical. A woman shrieks
and you think someone is being murdered in the mass.
A man holding a joint slowly smiles and shows how
hysterical is the outrage.
Why do I write all this?
I don't need to convince you I am writing something
stable.
This is our society, your society, and I have not been
invited to the stage.
I jumped on the stage naked, dancing, waving my
genitals at the history you've forgotten.
The history you don't know.
Political geniuses work in every profession of this
country and they need a rebel man stating the obvious
they overlook. The obvious is there in their kitchen sinks,
in their malcontent continuing contentedly,
in their poisoned water. In their blessed politics.

※

Because businessmen make deals
a patriot conforms
follows orders
   murders and dies
while scoffing at a patriot
who burns a draft card.
Judgment requires no skill.
I am practicing no skill.

※

Hear me migrants from any land!
Do not come here!
Their lies are the plan!
This place is a zoo
and the morals are painted
on the cages of catastrophe.
They are willfully ignorant,
willfully cruel,
and because I care for you
I say, stay away!
Go somewhere the sun shines true,
where the caribou know who is truly subdued.
For the wreckage of the hateful, it subdues their hearts
into a mire of slime and subduing their vision of art.
For they are selfish and fearful
seeing so small.
The promises you've heard were never here at all.
You've met the bullies. Don't go
where the bullies make their home.
Some are trying, but none can agree
on how to make this world truly free.
While we're raging in a liar's land,

go around and avoid the disaster at hand.
Few of us know
how simple the solution.
Difficult is the mental pollution
of the loud, belligerent, hypocritical tools
who do not see the one absolution.
They will not hear. They will not see
because they are dying of impoverished souls,
of yelling and displacing.
How can they be happy who spread hate and lies?
How can they be happy when burning their eyes?
How can they smile
when insisting on their own demise?

Field lights and a wind which drowns
out voices
we don't need.
Smiling is all we need.
On what do we feed?
Not friendship?

※

New spring
      singing birds.

Some are going to disintegrate in their own
  cruelty.
Leave the muck at the lake bottom.

    Our home is upon the mountains.

※

They say they are all one
while jeering and proving
they are enemies.
They shout calm lessons in morality
at each other
over the river.
Some stand on the bridge serenading.
One side claps. One side boos.
Along come the free
going along the river
watching these angry tribes.
 Modern man fights phantoms
   manufactured
from his comfortable couch
vowing to destroy
invisible enemies.
The hypocritical political statement is
I don't want to hear it unless
it affirms what I want to hear.

※

Must be shunned.
Must be remade.
Time doesn't move.
Time does not exist.
Sociality changes.
A guard is placed in the park where we played and rode
our bikes.
We ride our bikes and there is a man hired to chase us,
yelling.
We've been here since before you, sir
and you will not drive us out.
We laugh and ride as he chases. No purpose but the
killing of fun.
We laugh. Our rebellion is simple. The Gael love
good trickery. Good humor.
All in good humor, even killing you we say,
Ah, we'll see you there in the otherworld.
Our ways are laughing, haughty joy, kind,
malicious, energetic, and happy.
Who can keep the freedom of timelessness? Only us
children who live in the bosom
and care and love and free your daring retrograde from
our will.
We have no need
of your ignorant rifling and squabbling over empirical
trades.
Ours is to live. Breathe. Smile. Construct our seeking
in magic everlasting.
Our home is temporarily this world. Our home is the
realm within.
We have no fear of your worries.
We are raised on bravery and regarding heroes
and majestic monarchs.

※

No delusion of endings
This is the ongoing
Seeking an ending is like
trying to sift and catalogue
grains of sand on the beach
while the surf is splashing your feet

※

  Bursting with ideas
   grinding to a halt
 stifling

※

In the blacklisting free country,
I care what you think is good,
but fuck off.
I am free and in any world,
even a government touting its freedom,
I write what I want and what is true.

※

The reason to rouse themselves.
Their scorn seeps through the windows
over the fences into the peace.
Where peace lives uninhibited,
why would I not love my home beyond?
We were raised with the freedom
in which our parents and grandparents let us roam
while we are survivors of genocide.
In these days, fanatics rule society in all ways.
Hipsters and their loving marches.
Loving elders disgusted at the young.
The young parents who need to get drunk to find their
poetry.
The high thinkers, criminals.
We have all the freedom to love
and all the scorn in our separation.
A California boy who thinks the buffalo are extinct
must travel to Wyoming to work for a woman who
doesn't love him, yet is carrying his baby soon to be
dead,
to find the herds greater than he imagined
alongside the rancher's gigantic ostriches.

※

Choke on the wine with your fearlessness.
Smoke the self-satisfied cigar.
On the sandbar with your rum and margaritas
you can manicure your scruffled hair,
but it grows back uglier.
I was raised in the most superb suburban comfort.
I can tell you, my clan breeds rebels.
The privilege we had gave us the thought and the want.
Some were too intelligent to conform.
Perhaps this was only where crazy kids are born,
but I believe
it carries on from the madness of beauty and imagination
over a worldview.
Above the wanting.
Below the ivy-league by choice and inclination.
Artists. Mad. Happy.
Torn up by the roots generations into growing.
Planted around the sunny south shores,
moving and given villages on avenues and cul-de-sacs.
For some of us, no fathers.
Raised by mothers and grandparents
and uncles and aunts.
Marriages destroyed in their selfishness
and saviors running and raising children
in the aftermath of the aftermath.
Still running and needing a new renewal of the simple,
unrecapturable values.
Why not drink? Give yourself a seizure with art.
Television families breathing
in their raptured respectability. It is scary how
mesmerizingly all
can reach nowhere. Sad. Farm dreamers
and social, industrial graves
from living rooms to tombs. Our parents
needed to break away

and we are drifting in the space of this caring need.
The abyss- looks like love, but it's not
-envelops eager emotions,
takes what can be recycled,
and our pointless needs and concerns are turned over
into the right point of origin.

※

I'll keep with the wisdom of children
keeping away from politics
When the adults are talking of bullshit
the children tune out and tune in to the music
and this is where I'll be travelling

※

When the morning was yet early, there was already
a teasing fight over food, a bike crash, and a wasp sting.
We procreate insanity and insane effort is required.

※

I don't know
might be the right answer, might be the wrong answer.
Too sure is knowing what is by nature uncertainty.
Unsure, yet willing to make a try.

※

In the desert, a beautiful, slow, poetic disintegration.
Doom makes my son laugh. I've got to keep his
enthusiasm.

※

Simple to condemn what you see as a bad act.
What is more interesting and takes more effort
is to wonder.
Does fate give us these choices? Does fate torture us
with these illusions of choices?

※

To unexpectedly catch your love
in an embrace with another
is more than enough to destroy a person's heart.
My heart has been destroyed many times.

※

Missing the mark is not committed
by running away from what you don't want.
It is not committed
by holding to read what you want to read.
Fear is sin. Running in fear. You fear,
you sin.

※

I have heard you in the day, nightingale
your voice as in place as a tree.
Your singing in the night, I love
and I am here for you.
I love you.
We nightingales
must keep our loose connections.

※

She claimed he put her on a pedestal.
He lifted her up to the pedestal by his side
and did not leave her. He was with her always.
Looking around at the beauty and wonder
and trying to show her and share it with her
and she was looking down at all those who could
suddenly see her
and she leaped down to them, leaving him,
and he pulled her back up
and she kept leaving.
Every time, she took a piece of his heart with her
in her sharp-nailed grasp because she was too afraid
to go alone and she knew he was hers.

※

The writer bleeds into your wallet.
Do you treat it as dust?
Do you feel?

※

I've had too much love with no love
Somewhere a French woman is lighting her own cigarette
needing a tryst like descendants of Scota need
to build and roam.

※

Murder for business, repeat false slogans.
About as much sense a blind nationalist can handle.
Invade and murder and claim your righteousness.
When they defend themselves, call them terrorist.
Propaganda is the destruction of information.
Governments cradle their citizens in whatever ignorance
it needs for control.

※

The children run
The fanatics cling to guns
And my child reads my eyes
And asks if I'm alright

Read child, to learn the difference
Of holocaust and hollow-not
And ride the neverending waves
And search for answers none can find

Don't stop, the weather calls
For bravery and allocation
And some are taught to dwell unheard
And yell their empty unheard words

Right the wrong of mischief
And mastery

※

A river of anger
  will take you to where
    you don't belong
It is the fastest route to
  missing your fate
It is the way the enemy feeds
  The enemy is everything which
    isn't for your joyful life
Every time you speak in anger
  you are lost from sight
    and the world within you falls
      into a horrid plight
Never can the answers find
  you when your mind is lying
You must quiet the dreams in laughter
  and refrain from dying

※

      I saw a star become brighter and brighter until it disappeared and was gone, but I could see it wasn't gone. No one was watching it anymore. They turned to find some other. I tried to get them to look, to see there could be more. But, they were not listening, they were gawking and pointing elsewhere. So I looked, and looked longer, until I could see swirling light within the darkness.

※

All the flicks of a lighter
trying to make the sparks hold source
seeking that good moment
and when at last the fire stays
amidst the air
        the sea
the calling is there
and is romantic

※

In the old ways we can travel the dark and light and laugh and not be stuck.

※

How much my silence was misinterpreted, why would I speak?
I kill ignorance in myself and pray for everyone's excellence.
Not power.
My sympathies reach.

※

You will not see me unless you know how to search.
I see the beautiful child running.
I see modern man's righteous disdain.
The palm trees are shaking off
what is not needed in the breeze,
the mountain sound through the trees
is calling
here.
What can be done is undone
and we do it anyway
to keep our rightful place in the living.
Go where you want
and don't go where you do not want.
Don't be afraid when the world flips over on you.
Anger is fear.
I think of the gone lovers,
the conversations we won't ever have.
We do not need these conversations
which are the past.
I see a beautiful, open world with no flags
where the flowers are rising.
A dove flies, and a dove's baby egg
is shattered on the sidewalk.
Someone's morning started with death
and nature goes on moving.
Walk away from the dry scent of wrong.
The pomegranate flowers are growing on the bush;
some are laying on the pavement
still beautiful.
They will live on.

※

Cleaning the gutter of his drugs
and fixing the lid in a rush
at the demands of foreigners who don't know him
and don't know what he's doing
he gets a ride and the driver disappears at a step

He gave life's virginity to vampires
who cared less about him
than about their french nail glitter

We'll put aside the cruel
and move to the ignorant
they are comfortable in their cemented worlds
and when something is not accepted
it is wrong
sidestepping thought for self-assurance
no matter how blockaded by lack

Unconditional openness
and the will to have sharing conversations
the colors are important in the old ways
the unique is not feared, but embraced
what you do not know
you can learn
what is new is exciting
a chance to expand
not insist your protective shell is all there is to the world
Where would we be without liars and thieves?
Where would we be without those who fear?
Happy

Slaves and liars pretend to be savage
using words to label their repetitive wastefulness
the wildman's heart trembles at being called a savage
because he is a heart who cares

Jesus became a rebel, and he might be speechless
at the authorities which call his name
at all those who believe a good person is one who kills
whomever the government tells them to
and don't realize, don't care, don't fathom,
want not to know it is business
and not protection
it is a show of wanting more and convincing others to
risk their lives for it
and condemning and convincing others to condemn those
who do not want
our children to die for greed
ignorance and lies are strong conductors
too much beauty is wasted on these
labels for the insecure

※

Poets' minds touch each other
without first reading
what they've read

Put a mop on the head
of your guru

※

Elf branch swords
script of heroes
in the hillwood
adventure
of timeless protection
exploring and saving
our tribe
who was lost among the tribeless
having lost our language
regaining our visions of reference
among many tribes
melding
and loved or disdained
for retaining their language
and ways of gathering
in our voyage of relearning
to make the best of hand and wing
of mind and heart singing
the storylines sharing
and growing in caring
to original truth
of savoring

※

You are my shakespearean love
not the tragic ruined kind
but the nostalgic beautiful kind
pink dove and black raven
two wanderers found each other together

※

The bright attitude seeing a couple
making love on the roof
is not what those through the window probably is.
I'd be happy for their love
and even for their possible love
or their base spinal primal grinding.
It all connects.
There is a need
and I am happy for those who are living.
The civilization of not looking away
and being offended is absurd
and we must live with this
while we are what we are
and alive in our starry sight
unapologetically.
You in the stars
is the closest I've been
in ages
to a dreaming truth.

※

My speaking is silence.
A hero is not someone
who kills, but protects.
How do you correlate invasion and murder
with defending freedom?
Civilization is a threat.
Conform the proper amount.
We cage wild animals.
We'll cage a wild person.

※

Winning terrorists
They won without doing anything
They won because you are zealots
They won because you decline your history
They won because you elected them
They won because enough of you
talk way too much
These are, maybe, the final say
I shall have on your suicidal society

※

shut ears
breed big mouths
not necessarily with anything to say
but granted the privilege from the universe
to say as much as they can
with what breath they are given
perhaps, it is a depository of useless
serenity to listen
conversation
granted in places
where intelligence
can contemplate in silence
while the utterances of conceit
contract inanity spreading
and dissipating
at the circumference, this ego-mania
not allowed
to maneuver into precious beauty
keep your righteousness
and your foul heated temper

※

The happy anarchist watches
and wishes to explain
which in simple poetry
is poetic in disgrace
the need these intentionally ignorant
excusers do not ignore
yet abhor.
Do you say you do not care
when we are poisoned and drowned
in waste?
Your vehemence has no merit.
You pander off the discussion.
The ruler you howl for
is the neglected bully.
When he punches someone in the face
you say
don't be too sensitive.
When abusive actions bring disgust
you cry
why are you searching hurt
upon our poor baby?
Those who behave
as if the world began
two hundred and fifty years ago
with nothing in between
which they should repair
wish to be the
sole inheritors of freedom.
When you are disrespectful
you say
they can't handle the truth.
The truth, you yellers
is we can
maim, murder, destroy
righteously in this flag's employ

happy to disregard the death
when orders mean more to you than a child's breath.
You are not men when you are this blind.
Foolish schoolyard cliques being towed by cruelty
with morals admittedly for sale
as long as you know where to pay
to appease they who have disposable conscience.
The country whom you do not know
lest you know
how we came to where we are
you'll die for
when they say you must die.
To be grown and trusted with your mind
they have not granted you.
Yet, for them who are paid to decide
you'll malign nature's tide,
sarcastic, snide, smug; subside.
They want a country of healthy
young corpses.
The rulers howl
their innocence
and when they howl their lies
and guilt of proof
you pat them on the head
and shield them with
finger-pointing other-blaming.
Look anywhere but at our faults.
Why are you so intent
on holding our ruler accountable?

The universe is letting ignorance
have a field day.

※

Music and pizza
Are maps to
Peace

※

The old ways believe in possibility without being ruled by it. We call ourselves by our honored ancestors and live as we are. The word pagan is not a pagan word; it is what the religious call us. We are free. When you become less than a person, you call yourself a religion.

Believe in goodness

※

I see some smiles and many downcast faces,
more swaying sad souls.
Brothers are shouting on the sidewalk
about how bad life is.
"Every day it is worse!"
Their doomsday signs are painted with fire.

We are eating sushi and loving
and going to the bookstore to explore
and kiss in the labyrinth.
Kissing you is breathing.
Breathing your breath
is electrified truth.

Children on the stony hills watch.
Do the adults care?
One kicks up dust
and they see hope.

I've been to where the Lorax
lifted himself away,
over the snakehole civilization,
past the mountain dragon sleeping,
climbing the rope above lion caves
to a stone ring on a spired summit.
I'll show you.

The town is going to sleep.
The town is waking up.
A lull in reality,
a refreshing neutrality.

The dirt farmers are riding home
from their thankless thoughtless trades;
the fumes, the dust, a grave display.

Those who require policing
are thankful for the gossipy radars
scanning their boredom.

We are dissonant synchronicity

Mother Earth is needing
the orgasm we don't give her
when we take.

※

You're disrespecting the land!
We, sarcastic and laughing,
know what is good.
Those who stamp the earth
with concrete, who suck its blood
and melt its bones
to keep in prison vaults,
make false preservation engineered.
A fat, shiny man yells
"I'm on the edge! I can't go any further!"
The native silently points the way right beside him.
The man who would not go near the ornery horse
says, "Don't let him paw the ground.
Don't let him eat the scrub."
  "Why?"
The man goes away with no good answer.
The native whispers to his wild friend,
  "You can do whatever you want."

※

They're all the same who have always been here.
You have one friend
among this mass of moving figures
who invited you to play the piano
then everyone disappeared.
The piano is gone.
The place it had been
is replaced by a jukebox inserted in the wall
and a giant tv above.
Where the old jukebox had been
is replaced by an atm.
They're all the same who have always been here.
Figures.

※

they drive
pointless
pacing
policing our homes
with no thought of more than why
wasting expensive energy

※

The world has had enough
faux christians
faux news
faux noses turned away
devoid of thinking.
It will renew wisdom
boiling up
until it explodes
and rains peace
in the seeking and
exploration of truth.

※

walking in the rain
looking up into the trees
I am here
I am not here
there is no I am
we are not meant to be mortal
the birds are singing happily
   the rain washes everything into view
the moving water
the change which is not change
we are kin to all
release
there is only one of you
   be a child

※

You climb the tree
and everyone leaves you.
You have the tree, the air,
privacy.

※

I am the rider of a chaos dragon
and I always knew
I am the friend of the forest dragon
a child of seafoam and light
and I sit with faeries of the dew
and watch the blue heron in the slough
and in the tide, the upside-down fish will prove
who I am and all I've seen through

※

You have made slaves
and you keep slaves
the precious is dead to you

Silence is finished

※

Our minds are not for hurling in noise.
Talk is an art, a pastime, not a necessity. Talking leads
to all the trouble.
I'm sitting on perfection
ready for spring.
You've been smoking this plant
not even knowing what it looks like,
eating this food
not knowing yet what they've been eating.

Their big lie is crumbling.
I am sad for what this world has become.
I am happy for what the world is becoming,
because the world becomes what we decide.

The roots- look up
we are the roots below and above.
This middle ground teaches us
we are
in the center of life.
I grew up talking with flowers.
I was taught they are friends.
They will listen.
Listen to them.
What good is anything without flowers?
Seeing flowers grow.
Seeing wild water move.
Seeing pipe smoke
drift over the pond
like mist
and knowing
in the smell of wet earth
in the sight of shovel and axe
you are making life grow.
Nature gives

and you are nature.
I belong here.
This holy ground
because it has been made holy
with true sight.

The jasmine will return
with happy customs,
not of keeping
but of play.
The home, simple
and resolute
in being.

Seek your ancestors.
You may speak with them,
for you are connected by immediate blood.

※

A man in a machine clumsily doing what many men could do
faster with cooperative finesse.

※

With no time for reply or discussion,
they'll retract loyalty
from those who refuse
to casually connect parents and children
as deportable criminals and invaders
with no guiding information.
Invaders: those fleeing desperation?
Invaders: those who invade, murder, point fingers
and yell at others for believing their promises.
Invaders: those who tell everyone to appease them
on their stolen land and throw immigrants out by the hair,
inheritors of genocide and slavery
in a nation raped by ignorance yelling
about those trying to sow seeds in corrupted opportunity.
The distinct characteristic of American hypocrisy,
they welcome invasion
wafting it like a degenerating fume
with loud voices and the intentional disuse of the mind.

※

a warrior is born
it is no solace

there is no death
we live

the drums howl
the strings beat

I feel your unsaid
Love

I'm seeing all
the deaths of my grandfathers

※

I am the rocky hills
I am the mountains
I am the Sun
I am the Sky
I am the Sea
I am the space between
I am the mystery
when the ravens agree
courting on the spring cool breeze
smiling silently
I am the gifts I bring home
I am the desert sage
I look and see
  it is all bigger
I am the giant tramping the hills
  to farther than anyone knows
I am taking out the pen abrupt
I am the trail which was once not
  and shall be no more
I am the
   wild no trail beard
I could have driven but I chose
   to walk
I came to feel
   not to miss
I came to be
  not pass by
I am a handful of sand
I am a child
  in love
I have found her
I am the circle
I am happy

※

Every day you write a poem is a good day
The poet hears from the universe, and speaks
He must sit outside
  to write
  to heal
everywhere is as much the soul
as the sun warming
the body reviving
you feel the technology sickening
and you must have no fear to say
this is not good
  you must put it away
and go outside

The real celebrity
  is the Sun
  the sky
  the trees
  flowers
  the ragged beautiful hills
    the breathing

The debris sinks into the earth
packs in
the earth rises
it is moving
the mountains eroding are also rising

The rake which rends the pond
is nature
and the anger at change
is dislocation from nature's way
the breeze breathes truth

※

The rain heals us.
Clears all.
Low clouds are skiing the hills
up the mountains
to the sky.
The wild clouds are
misty warriors.
Kill your mind's
lies.
Walk with your heart.
Rage, howl against the false.
Be alive and fly.
The phantom caution which has no reason
but the fear of your love being taken away.
How it connects?
It has no reason.
Write until your fear is drowned in love,
freedom,
seeing.

※

The desert houses
 cluttered in futuristic silver junkyards
 of nostalgia
Good ol' days were never gone
 and never arrived
The lone wolf teaches and feeds his pups
 and he needs the wild sea
 solitude's big mountains
 open valleys of travelling and far-seeing
The hunger brings him near
 to the civilization
 to edges of ranging
 near to those who
 would fire upon him
 raging and indifferent to his existence
He must find the sustaining world
 for his clan
 and dare the reality
The takers have sucked away
 the unseen wilderness of seeing
 unseen, tearfully seen
 by a tribe of wild, unrelenting freedom
The dinosaurs wandering these wide valleys
 guarded the holy silence
 which has not been
 since their time
 which they would rumble and obliterate
 and which would then return
We must attend the necessity
 be aware
 and fight for the food of our life
 while we stay

※

    The pine smell, the earth and the sap, immediately brings me back.
    I need the kindness of trees.

    A kind soul frolics toward me
stating her mediated fears, a new military
challenge in her mind, asking what I think.
    I ask why to know why
and say I'll love her no matter what she does.
    I do not ask why in a blank judgement,
though perhaps she thinks I do.
    Perhaps because she has been raised by surrounding judgement.
    Or she knows why I ask,
an innocent question.
    Perhaps I think she may think otherwise
because how often I have been in the midst of judgmental ignorants
    who couldn't know me
    and don't wish to know.
    See how pain could poison conversation
with the residual stabs from those who talk
but do not converse?
    Words of tools,
words of serving a country.
    I don't serve.
    Give me a thought you have, not conceived
from television and movies, and we can have a talk.

    Back to swords in the woods. Back to fantasy's reality.
    Truth
    and the breeze of joy.

※

Your little white house
so you can spill red
for the flags
making the clear water into mud

   When we die, is it for the height of becoming licensed
commodity?
Dark bright storm
whom you know
yet know nothing of

※

You have a magic mirror.
With it, EVERYONE you look at
has your face.
You have everyone's face
when they look at you.
You are reflected
wherever you go.
How are you treating yourself?

※

On the air
I smell autumn has arrived.
Called back to the pagan dreaming
I pass the old places
where I've vomited, where I've loved
and the memory of those who've lied
is more a memory than a hurt.
They spoke falsely
with all the conviction
of one who will never be questioned.
I am free of them.
One seagull in the desert
makes me smile at the newer old
and I return.
Around I go
home to the one
who reminds me of true love.

※

I don't regret any day
I spent in fantasy.
All the days I'm still living
in the breeze of far-off dreaming
is beyond measure
of the real,
never kills
and forever healing.

※

The Moon cannot be captured
  it is poetry
  it is experience
  the eye of our mother

The horses run with me in the morning
  every shade
  every color
  to the edge of the fences

The talk is eventually meaningless
  to listen is to learn
  to listen brings us closer
  until our arrival lives as ours

※

I cast away
   the crutches
 I mistook for legs
and ramble on
 mysterious giving
   of souls
     I left the rooms
       where unknowing compounds
     where they stare at their hands
and defend viciously
  their useful unliving

※

for the poor European Americans
who'll never know Maya Angelou
for the dreams I must recall
and cast into the abyss of reading
to be read
to be adored
to be sanctioned and abhorred
here may you rest your sorrows
and listen for a while
to the realms and dreams of a man
exasperated
the wild animals in the zoo
big beyond any
the wildest
they will protect you
from the danger
you know but do not know what it is
while you're looking
they'll die in the resistance amalgamated
pierced by endless arrows

※

A dappled skull in the street on the way

Repeat your soundbites
Retard your thoughts
With clipped learned language
Arguing with the soundbites in your head
Not listening to what's actually said

In the dunes I will forget the hurt from those not here

You don't get to talk to us
Until you undo your desertion
Those who abandon their family
Do not have the privilege of trust

I am waking up and resting in one moment

Bloody backlegs mangled into the road
A bunny looking frantically for its family
Its ears moving, it cannot crawl
Tethered in torment to its demise

※

the rain held the warmth in
until yesterday returned
when I smelled a nostalgic best
and thought of a way to return myself
and then in a few breaths returned
to the here and now
for we enjoy memories
but are so quickly delusioned by them
as I noticed again later
desperately holding to an escape
when I smelled a nostalgic time and place
I have need of escape from
though I escaped
our potential is constricted by our
misunderstanding
our only true option is fearlessness
with intelligent thought
and spirit travel on our journey
our battle is found after we discover
theirs are unworthy and dishonorable
and ours are within ourselves and
against the average
in the governments of a swarm
we break free to be
the artist

※

Lost my train of naught

The mountains don't need your words. When we speak, even when it is to each other, it is to ourselves, the one being we are always connected in. Be aware of how you speak and what you say.

※

What we can express through full self-control
is a rising to the summit
of our seaward life.
Lir tells the true,
'Do not go there - I will take care of it'
and the ocean will rise to cover the enclosure
while rejoicing are those who value freedom
above entertainment
and the trapped will simply swim up and away
to rejoin the home that's been denied them.
If you think we all cannot learn and relearn,
look to your own learning.
Go to the wide libraries. Go to the wild
and go to societies gathered in giving.

※

This son of the Sea
knows the Great Tree beckoning
and will carry the love to where the wide land ends

※

Giving! Doing for others
is a way to find happiness.
Giving in thanks is the certain truth of escape
from self-centered thought
to the righteous good,
acceptance of gathering the world
to express it.

※

In the true house of the Spirit
an arch of sunlit trees in a forest
and we go through the open door above
to see through
where on a train moving fast along the mountain edge
one miserable passenger looks
at the dark rocky cliff beside
and another enraptured in exploration
looks in wonder
at the wide unmapped sunny world

※

From the Sea
we are born
to explore
to believe
We dance in the sky
and we see
the Great Song
our story
From the Earth
to the ones who bore me
I remember my mothers
and I am free

We wolves are driving away
　from the excess
　　the end

Ravens Courting

The morning when you feel what you must do
and you do it.
I sit outside in the air almost cold
in the rising sun
days before Samhuinn.
The birds are singing, gathering and feasting.
I see a hummingbird, its crimson and gold close
and it flies to move circles with its true love.
The swooshing louder than ever before
of two ravens up for a morning glide.
Doves come in twos and singles
to where the seeds are bountiful.
The projections of the angry
onto everything beautiful
is what we can release and discard.
They'll say the birds are not singing, they're fighting
and they're not kind as you would believe.
The songs you wish to hear, they'll say
are merely projections of fantasies.
I have seen birds giving, I have seen them kind,
I have seen them protecting each other.
If one more need we have before we waken,
I'd say it is to take your dreams and make them good.
I'd say it is to awaken what's true and see
we are the makers of reality
and beyond projections we live happily.

※

Walking the red brick path
through a forest tucked away
amidst starlight guiding
shadows of searchers and lovers
I gave you the shoe
of the tale of our joining
and a ring of a royal woman
and we talked as we had
when we walked in the hills
to begin this holding of hands
and we returned
to the happiest place on earth
where the fireworks greeted our coming

※

Remember how lonely you were without her
You won't remember until you feel it
Meditation with a pen
The yellow Sun in the sky
whereby looking out to the fantastic dream
you don't forget to look in and live the dream

An Irony of Cats

An irony of cats
they hate water
but love fish

What would they do
to bring them a question
beyond their dichotomy?

※

The more apparent the truth
   the more violently ignorance will enforce
     its right to exist
All civilizations are destroyed by greed
I was taught to brush away 'ism's
   to disregard labelling
 in favor of self-education
Where are your contrivances which have done well?
   none have succeeded
Only the free savage
   in his care and his heart
who has no ruler
   can say what civilization is
Only the kind and gentle soul
   who learns to direct his anger
     inward to realization and usefulness

On the Island

Always be happy and throw your thanks into the sea
When your dreams are flyin' away you can reconvene
on the island where we sing
You don't need anyone to tell you how to be free

To the brave belong all things

When we know we're going on the hero's road
we will prevail
We can laugh and dance away from their fear
of their own hell
We're on the island of the Well
My mother taught me the ancient ways
I'm listening through the shell

To the brave belong all things

Outside of time's barriers we exist
Oh we know Life must be kissed
We're from the island of the mist
Come with me and we will make a holy tryst

To the brave belong all things

※

Butterflies fly as they will.
Why are we so full of joy when we see them alive?
Much is bright and beautiful which
does not give us this feeling.
We feel the way we feel when they are close
because they are truly happy.
I've lived on an island on the Sun
in the sky above the Earth.
I've seen the sky's shifting
shading memories
and daily living.
I saw mountains unseen.
I saw someone who had been there, somewhere.
I swore I'd never work in the chain,
but this morning as I drove through,
the young woman was smiling and so kind.
It barely matters what you do,
but how you do it.
I've never done any job as happily as she.

※

a dirt road
one looks on disapprovingly
as the car drives faster
slightly speeding and kicking up dust
but then they hear him singing Africa
at the top of his lungs to the music
and they smile and forgive
he rides the old ways
searching for a new place
in the past-visited places
one of the unkind teachers from his school years
is hiking with her friend
along a trail above
and unhappily looks
as he passes
he looks back to see them turned
in derisive scowls
Go there ? he hears
and doesn't want to
and doesn't
a moment of pulling to the side
to let a car continue its way
and it is another white-haired lady
but she is smiling like life itself
is a joke
and waves
and they pass on by
sharing their positives
the hills appear in a new angle
thoughts about the past
infiltrate the happy mind
then are washed away
by the determination of the present
the right place is found
for breathing

where the butterflies are flocking
regardless the desert
many flowers are still blooming
and they remain
the many birds, a brightest yellow
made brighter by their darknesses
the horned caterpillars
which he takes account of
for he knows his children will be interested in them
seen in the pushing walk of the interest
the ripples in the current of the ocean
stands of trees
not isolated
but forming a wider forest to explore
the lion's mane in the breeze
its reflection in a window
remembers its humor
our pride is not in the self
it is in the tribe
the wider one can reach
the greater belongs its pride

※

a world
  a not-world
    pictured
leading us into a black-hole
  addiction of distraction
while the living who need us
  look on
the world alive
  lives on
and the dead
 are not even there

※

Your happiness
  your complacency
your fear
  are what they use
to steal your lives
  and make you murderers

※

I have to go to the quiet
listen to the quiet
the mountains rise in silent accord
the trail is louder
the wild has what we need
new green expands in rain
alive to its purpose
beginning last night
the hills rise higher
we go where we need
the feathery seeds
the rain encapsulates them
the blue-tailed baby rabbits
 are not as fast as they think
    but, fast
I've already been on the trail too long
I need to go to the quiet

※

White butterflies playing around the garden bench
   and on, creating a tickling breeze
birds in the woodworker's shop
   in the nostalgic music
a whittler smiles
a day comes for grasping the torch
and planting it in the ground
   here, sit, listen to the stories
and from here may be your port of adventure

※

We need poetry more than ever
   because bullies are picking fights
 and getting their supporters to commit
   to murder
 while yelling about defense
 louder than anyone with sense
   can be heard
We need a way to kill hypocrisy
   with fictional characters
     who are bigger
   than these tiny, self-absorbed
    crooks

The gods are tired of your shit
   this caravan
     of ignorance

※

Think about before
 You may say the universe
   has a beginning and an ending
 but it is not true
   Eternal continuance
   is ending and beginning
 You may see a wave ending
   but it is not so
 The wave is still there
   from ages ago
 When Achilles walked on the shore
   contemplating
  before his rage erupted
 those waves are still there

Before the Big Bang
   there was a universe
 and they had lives
 and lived, and pondered
 What ancient wisdom
   did they find
 and lost, renew again
 Where did they see
    where no longer exists
  what did they hear
 They were us

※

He was limping, dancing, one leg
in a splint,
praying on the hill.
I was happy to see him walking, unstopped
by an injury.
I waved, his long black hair
and face now seemed familiar.
Raising his hand, "Morning."
"Morning."
"Good day for a walk, hey?"
"Yes, it is."
"It's beautiful."
Heard his prayer
the sound of a drum,
an eagle, the earth
and a man walking his path.
Hi ya ya hweyah ha ho ha ya
I recognized this and turned,
"Hoka Hey!"
"Hoka Hey, brother!"
Then the triumphant
high-pitched yells, victory,
sending a jolt up one's spine.
He continued singing, praying.
I continued walking up the hill
into invisible curves of the land.
Living among a tribe which isn't my own,
the touch of my tribe brings a smile and calling.
We can go back from the beginning of accomplishment.
We can go farther,
beyond weakness of inaction,
and find truth of movement,
the truth of feeling,
the truth above ourself.
A hawk doesn't need to say it is free.

It is itself.
We are related to all.
There are some spirits who are kindred,
who help each other grow.
It is a tribe
aside.

The Lone Wolf and the Black Bear

Brothers
who jestfully gave pranks and battles
who explored the world
who fought each other
with unheeded anger
but when an enemy appeared
none defeated them
they're loyal, rare wild souls
the strong in their heritage
the king and warrior
of ancient lore
and sea-born druid champions
of seeing and fighting
learn to walk the world
in love and bravery

※

The fog and brick
 birds of the alleys in the heights
   of vaulted architecture
the dancing art
 of children
   of their ancestors
 signing with active hands
   give us peace
You are the lifeline

※

You can toil
   and they won't see it
You can achieve
   art, enlightenment - and still they won't see
   past their noise which
   they're passing as talk
uneducating masses shunning education
   decrying solutions
   regurgitating arguments
yet having none of their own
   can blame their scapegoat
   with ease and a laugh
while claiming coincidence
when they don't want to believe
and at their anger of your right
they will attack you

※

I want to be home
I am home
the smell
the jasmine and sunshine
and the sea
go and be where
the soul is at peace
the jasmine scented butterfly
in a morning song
the day rising in cloudy calm
a raven caw
a father smiling

※

In the violent rhesh
I splash the sea on my face
　no one will see my tears
I am shy
I have always been shy
I will always be shy
I am a man of the isle
　a man of the western sea
I am the very crying
of the need to make me writhe

※

palm tree in the sunrise
friend in silent joy
above the turmoil
aware

※

Mother Danu said,
 'Today, I will remind my children
  of their priorities.'
On the day of birth
for a princess of light,
 on the day of freedom's celebration,
  we are reminded the universe
 is not in our control.
The ground
  tossed us around like the sea.
 There is no stability.
This time, should your land on the coast
  be submerged,
you will not lose your history.

※

your gut vomiting its empty pain
reeling
realizing the hand you reach out to
isn't there
the forgetting
is why you're falling

※

morning wakes slow
in the open wooded hills

the birds are forever singing
the Sun alights on us like a play
the messages are here, everywhere

I am not who I was
save all the good

※

history and prophecy
music and poetry
full moon excellence
a bard is new and hoary

※

over the hills
through the rain
   to the forest of my imagining

※

They didn't know their own history
They laughed at their own language
it made me sad
  it made me angry
until I realized
 I am a teacher
  and they are the failed
  by their ancestors
who did not know
  there is no you
  without teaching
a culture dies
  when they don't learn
who they are and
why they are

Eight Eyes

I am speaking
of native conscience
in the sacred
science of spirituality
indigenous and diaspora
tap their empathy from nature's beginning
and the way of many views
connects the true histories
where heaven and earth
remain together
our responsibility
is shared in truth
continuing genocide and lies
have a militant empire built
your culture needs
guidance and honor
you are the ancestors
and must understand balance
to be a legend
to raise heroes
our homes have been desecrated
by the greedy and dishonest
and our lack of action
and now we must be wiser
what good is star wisdom
without earth wisdom
they are shared knowledge
in the accent of eternity

※

a path under which you grow
thinking your path
upon steps and narrow
is the path
but lo
above
is the path
a bridge overhung with
moss and trees
and there
the hidden land

Happy Anarchy

tempting fate where orange spider webs
which can match the sun for color
weave in the sea of teal

the guilty excess of civilization
must give way to the happy anarchy

break and crumble the sad temptations

make it an honest love
and honest calling
not armored by the sham

driven in greed and sensation
there is a tourniquet required for the heart

destroy with a smile the mad vexations

※

I live
on the edge of existence
no name could say
what I am
but writing
with the pen given to me
by the woman I love
I am

※

The Moon sliver
 sharp star above
  flying higher is a pink jetstream
 on a desert planet
Don't worry about
 who you are
Go forth living your family values
Let yourself out of your mind
 and into your soul
 non-worry over opinion
Only true
 only true
The Sun's pink plumes
 even when day
  is turning into night

※

autumn is the writer's spirit
the mythology
the cool air and slanted Sun
the breeze changing
reaping the harvest
of learning
happily culminating
the reflection of joy in a life's turmoil
as the ending year we draw near
to the darkness wherein
we are light born again

※

The material is anything but.
Energy, alignment, these are right to me.
Vision
Time does not exist; it never did.

※

Moon through the branches
I saw a fairy slip by

the real world is encircled by roads

a person walks out of their beautiful house
and closes the door
like it's nothing to them
not worth their love
and goes to jobs which teach us
our creative energies
are not as important
as how much the expenses drain from us
and in this unsympathetic impatience
with conformity to the bad system
I remember, not everything is what it seems

※

Travelling in the sunlight
seeing rabbits run
they played on the hilly tracks feeling
what they were imagining
searching to find the brave beauty
which sister was happy to learn
were sunflowers growing in the wild
amidst many thorn trees
and the relics of civilization
and what was thrown into a seasonal lake
to be moved by strongish wind
and then found
as they held hands on the way to childhood learning

I turned away from civilization's cement
and heard, 'don't go that way'
but I didn't want to walk where anyone could see
so into the scorching lake where I heard not that way
and kept walking to try to find a way through
and a thorn the length of terror stabbed
with my full weight into the center of my foot
I pulled myself from it
and held it not to let it defeat me
bringing it home to burn
and remembered my son's pierced heel
initiated into a life of warrior's pain
and thought of Mac Airt's Fianna
as I bled through the desert
It was one of their rites of testing
that a thorn in their heel while running be removed
without missing a stride

receive this as a knowing of the way
for it is our choice
to take the pain and satire and hurt
take them as occurring in our path
and not allow missing our stride

※

a raven has no need of your signs
no trespassing for the wild
I forgot my pain
Was there ever pain?
No
my hunger returned
Was there ever any hunger?
Yes
and no
There is nowhere
There is nowhere
only here is somewhere

a poet's ingredients

an overactive imagination
and a sharp pen
the morning is poetry
before reflection
it is remembrance

※

Give no attention
   to the haters
   what you are cannot be stolen
   they are nothing
   they will not be remembered
   they are shadows carrying on
   beneath the sun

a culture wanting to be part of something greater
   Sports, Enlightenment, Entertainment
   everything for what can be seen
   rarely in our own lives
   distracting ourselves with fullness
   tearing ourselves away from the silence
   while dreams sail away inspiring
   and dreamers sit on the shore
   exhausted

Get up!
   there's a hissing in New York
   calling you to replace your anxiety
   with all the best of your life
   live in your peace in the middle of fantasy
   our realm is a fine place to play
   it is our day

※

In accordance with the laws
we can unwrite, rewrite, consign
to the gods of death our flitting ideas

※

for ever a reckoned recall is stained
by the times of caring catastrophe
and we may divert and snuff out the remembrance
which is current and remains a pain which stabs us

for I am a man of another dimension and in realms ever
fleeting carry the waves to the hearts of the evening
where the ready and unready
wake in the dreams

I am not the only one kicking up dust in this morning yellow bright silhouette. Here I am, always drawn to the water, in the desert seeking the Light.

※

We had the connection
from this white flower at your feet
to the shrub it came from
but in the smiling pathways
of renewing
the trees are ripped from the ground
and their roots lay eviscerated
as from where they once stood
we can hear them screaming in pain
and now they are crying
'Do not live here-'
this place kills the growing
while evidence of life
is for aesthetics
with no care
of cruelty which yells at children
for climbing trees
Do not stay here
where thrives anger

Go where you can see
magic everywhere

※

We went to where
the sweet grass grows
for the blessed blend
our pagan ways
give us a kind of seeing
where the roads wash out to the oasis
and our tribe explored
the western lands
over and in the stream of learning
and we shared life
in the children's wild
until we returned
happily
to the wide open desert sea

Through the moonlearning
windows of speech
we wonder at the sky-fire clouds
and roll down the glass
to reveal all colors are there
the pink and orange
sunrise upon my sunflower's amazed face

※

      Today is the kind of day
I would not have gone to school
      the sunrise bursting lilac
and the scent of morning's cool
      I slipped into where I'm
meant to be and realize there is
      nothing ever truly wrong

※

breath from the mountains
with trees and snowy fountains
wolf paws contemplating the dawn
old twisted logs

a feeling is kneading your guts
and it's wrong
to waste away unregarded all along
while your reward to achieve your dream
is standing alive among mysterious spires

※

The morning explosions
in your desecrating freedom
waft away like a breath of unlearning
polluting as it goes
diluting in our bliss

Happy, find your place
don't worry about
what they want,
but this is not the question
What are you doing? giving
How are you caring for yours?
You're not, until you remember
who you are,
then you are
Are you enlightened
or do you think you are enlightened?
Who am I
to be thinking I'm enlightened?
What is enlightenment?
-He smiled, 'Yes'
Wonder…

destruction won't stop
the wringing hands of the fates
destruction is meant to have its counterpart
in creation
and any without this meeting is
clever terror

※

you are good

you found the forgotten spoon
which wisdom couldn't get to
visualizing, made you cry
the sea home
and abandonment
taught us to have our good daddy
who filled pages obliterating civilization
after creating the happy place
finding, yet having it desecrated
and eventually understanding
how he'd invited
to become sickhearted
from a lifetime of pain
mistreated
until she accepted him
and his true loves
met and smiled
the match healing
like seeds in sunlight
returning with the sight
a filled page
to reach the epic reminder
of the best vision
which sails where
we always dwelled
upon the need
eternal
and on the other side you see

※

tents on sides of freeway hills
and one-way highways
sharing is what I've seen
in the dirty, urinal-scented streets
and sidewalks
the hot breeze hints at where
the clean words pour free
and the woman is there

※

The mountains see the sunrise first
in their silence above
the small movings
a dusty sunrise
misting the dry morning
the cool air stays
and says, 'I'm here now,
it's time,
there is no more time.'
and what is good in your children
you keep
and watch them grow
and love them as pudgy babies
and cataclysmic guilt comes when you
hurt them by your anger's eruption
conscious or unconscious
is no remorse enough?
hold to this joy
walk light as leaves tapping through trees
and go right
the way you wish
not this way you've already gone

go a new way
and see a new happiness
you believe in the way for this
right living
you were happiest in the seclusion
while all the believing, not believing
is nonsense
a visible brightness
away from the lonely
to the illuminated dream
you have found
and must find yourself
within

※

The pond is almost completely drunk
by the hard rock soil and slate sharp sky
the geese are not gone yet
but are getting ready farther where the earth lifts up
to meet a horizon of detailed mountain silhouettes
and we must look here to what begins to grow

※

the bird call
from the impossible height
clear as the sentinel
the scent of green sagebrush blooming
cold, but the sound is warm

※

You are ruled by internet disconcerting
it is not your culture
it is a time sucking vulture
taking you away from your children and garden
and reminding you you've lost
what you've never lost
get away from your nightmares
and go to your true seeing
technology is only good for art
and art is only worth it if it is greater than
the artist
the cows in the rain have more art than
your picture
step out into the morning
see the poison lake and fumes
with your calm awakening
as the trees dance in stillness
ready, trembling
ready to burst with the budding
I heard a young wolf cry

I will be the soap
wash the saturation from your eyes

※

Don't wait till the next sunset

The sunrise wraps an arm around you
and you can live brightly
to create life

be the light
you want to be

something new is reflecting
below the dusty fog
new nostalgia of forward momentum

※

the darkness has always been
and the simple has always been truth
and when we say what we didn't intend to
it comes out much brighter
the children don't intend to be free
they are
and in imagination unsullied
there is freedom far away
from delusion's disconnect
into the immediate
of the real

※

Generations who will travel the Universe
have returned to remake
this world of dinosaurs
Cannibal culture
wears greed as a jewel in its cap
In this era
the poets rise
You'll be sad for all the literature
you didn't read
for the reminders you didn't write
and when the fight is here
in our inner sanctuary
reputable and possibly catastrophic
a poet is insane
and right to say truth
giver of honesty
poetry sees into eternity
which will inevitably rectify

※

empty rhetoric building the empire's
freedom of selfishness
pulling in the expenses
of their own health
and the right to be unrespectful
to their own goodness
refusing to understand themselves
a nation of uneducated cows
voting with all the misinformation
thrown like confetti in their faces
while establishment fights
to keep you thinking you're fighting the establishment
because if you were educated and healthy
it wouldn't be anymore
it would be something great
but lies jabber semi-coherently
and walk away
while a sooth is still packing its pipe
they don't care for your peace talks
the violent, genocidal swindlers
they know what they're doing
they take and see peace in taking
and others letting them take
they laugh as you sign their peace treaty
because they never meant it honestly
they're using its excessiveness
to make their lies seem like truth
and their promise of peace is their promise of war
they laugh and shrug
as they disregard their word
they have no honor
and so must keep their transitions written
to be traded, changed, and made irrelevant
rather than speak their lies too many times
and reveal themselves

they who do not even know their god's name
lost among their appropriations to convert you
Truth is not more complicated than truth
Untruth is a wicked simplicity
destructive and careless
the west wasn't stolen with guns
their winning was made of lies and murder
and theft in the night
to create a false view of might

※

Green- a flash!- green
the arriving meteor
it says, 'go, do what you must.'
I hadn't known at first what it said
it was speaking in star language

※

Had I done nothing,
   were I nowhere,
it would seem like all was
   a moment ago;
but I live.
Many are the memories,
   some of them so bad
   because they are so dull.
Why did I make those choices?
   Mental compliance, nothingness?
Why is my body aching in tiredness?
   Because I live in it,
   I vigorously love, I build,
   I surf, I remember to explore,
   I learn and more.
Dancing and singing every day
   is our regiment of joy.
I have found true love with my children.
I have found the match of my soul's searching.
I was always lonely.
   I'm not anymore.

※

hazy changing sunrise
the Dawn's Mother goddess
in my eyes
having seen through the earth
to the unending sky
the toad croaks, 'I'm looking'
the cows wander happily chewing
the birds whistle, 'Good morning!'

  Wake up and work for the mula you fool I hear rings at 3:30 won't get us a ring but I hustle this easy till home and a shower then wake up and take all the time in an hour I can to make daily this inspiration and give it to fools who don't see desperation they wander and whine about crime all the time but who is writing these lines on a dime it's a loner wolf calling to nowhere relieving his fellow wolf pack of the sheep drawing near then they cut down the trees and his forest is dwindling we've got to eat something and your mind tastes like dumplings
  A writer called Daddy he has nothing catty but truth in a game he never was playing he sings and he says not your praise do I need just set yourself on a high mountain and bleed till you see the promise of the calling homage to the radical dwelling of races and twigs and the barriers that I destroy to your fibs which hold sway of your own minds and the ken of your kids and I don't need a thanks or display of a shiv simply give it a moment to think and call dibs on yourself and be brave have the balls to feel and be real
  Then lunch rolls around you've been in reemergence and you sup and educate yourself to divergence from the normal behavior of bye folk to the depressing realization of my joke that all you see is everything wasting unless you can flow from your fear like a bee sting
  Because after what you want you must care first and make sure your life's revolutions are worth your children they're all that you need and your seething is nothing unless you can use it for feeding their brains who need a guiding father and mother to principle the one with the other so make time to make sure the time is well spent and never give up what was meant to be lent

※

young ponderer
in the freedom of aloneness
with the solitude of cats
learning the calm silence
raised in the otherworld
where dragons and unicorns dwell
which has always been more real
than the simulation
half inside our minds
half an energy-draining pie
we crammed the stories into potential
and now the first desk
is given in solitude
to someone who will use its continued probability
which has raised the upside-down fish
out of obscurity
from the unknown
into the world of story
which is all
for stories are meant to be told and retold
and their births reimagined
for the younger generations
and by the younger generations ever giving
their dreaming to the universe
which is dreaming through us
it is a parade of giving and receiving
a trading cycle of love
in the blissfully wrecked experience of living
where sometimes I am angry
at the burning of the Library of Alexandria
but then chuckle at myself
for I have the history
I am a bard
a keeper, finder, giver of stories
past, present, future

which is our ancestry
our heritage, our possibility

※

Make a bigger circle
continue its expansion
and never stop giving
the whole of who you are
in ever-increasing generous truth

The wild prince asked at the table,
"Is it your revolution?"
and the brave queen answered,
"It's us all taking care of each other."

※

The poet rocks in tears
Needing his ancestors
Meeting his tribe
Alone and found
And smiling through tears

※

Waves of light caught by the clouds
reaching up
if all were grey surface
we'd have no purpose

Need to affect the story
so intensely…
the Sun is clearer
though it's always been there

The air is pure
the birds are singing louder
more freely
as our noise and exhaustion cease

The peaks are returning
and seeing stars bring us home where
the Great Song
lives in nature's quiet

Life Under Water

Life under water is best spent without forgetting
when you breathe in life you are past wanting
I don't care what your point is, I don't want to fight
surfing, eating, singing, reading, making love all night
in the stars, in the waves, in my heart we are
together, together
We are together

I've been looking for joy, I've been looking for peace
I've been looking for her
wandering on the edge of the land alone
why don't I fly into the water and make my way
when you see happiness is always shown you can
be okay

write on, baby, write on
we'll find each other on the way to calling
with smiles and no fear
we'll meet my dear

Save me a seat on the bus home
and I'll meet you there
one hand made for another is the only way I care
to travel and honor our children
who look up and wonder
why the Sun and Moon are with them, for love

write on, baby, write on
we'll find each other on the way to calling
with smiles and no fear
we'll meet my dear

How Far I'm Loving You

Calling home around the tree
Calling home to my happy dreams
and I want you to see
how we can be
and how far I'm loving you

We've been treated wrong
and we've done wrong, it's true
and we can learn
to say when the light of day sees us coming in
we'll get our turn
to see how far I'm loving you

strummin' strings and cookin' our dinner
no fault we need pursue
we're livin' true
coffee in the morning with hugs and kisses
I'll be your man, you'll be my missus
and I'll set the mood to
how far I'm loving you

Carry You

When the world is rolling over
like a boulder
shaken off its roots
while we are getting older
I will write a song for you

I will carry you where we make camp
from Paris to Amsterdam
I will carry you along the California coast
to the land of the unknown

and when our league is dancing
and when they learn to fly
we will smile and say
it's a good life to be alive

I will carry you to our next camp
from Scythia to Japan
I will carry you along the California coast
to the land of the unknown

We don't have god or a devil on our shoulder
we have an old jedi telling us to be brave
when the stress gets colder
we will not fear any wave

I will carry you when the camps are gone
across the ocean to Avalon
where the California coast used to be
loving you eternally

※

In the strange spring
the kingdom of victory begins
where the fearless writes his rìghàrd soul
to release the world within
into this
and wholly connect
where the beautiful, brave, intelligent rìghan
and the league of children
druid healer and warriors
expel the darkness with their light

Daylight Murders

If a country is only as rich
    as its poorest citizen
you are starving, afraid, freezing.
    If a country is only as righteous
as its most debased criminal
    you are a murderer walking in the daylight
    patting yourself on the back, smiling.
If a country is only as free
    as it allows itself to be
you are existential exhaustion
in self-imprisonment.

※

I want to live my life in the sun
I don't accept being too tired to be awake
No dirt can touch me
I float on soles of light
We were made to meet, to have this date
luminary specks in a sea
since this universe was born to cite

※

Caution: a poet lives here
They are unpredictable
recklessly honest
and deafeningly silent

※

There is a flock of dogs pretending to be sheep.
There are flocks of sheep saying, yes, yes
when they're told what to think.
There are wolves lounging and playing in the forest
and the lone wolf says, Don't go to their game,
a lonely jest.
You may convince me for a time it is good,
but your prejudice is always understood
as a blight on the everlasting.
I won't ring the bell of your blasting.

※

It is a perfect sunrise
a perfect 75°
it is a perfect song of the birds
perfect mountains which are always alive
it is a perfect morning to be working
and growing in the world
to be giving
the sunlight is perfectly
lighting up the shadows

※

I thanked the Red God
this morning
and he said,
Don't thank me.
Go make poetry-
In his element
we can see more clearly
the Eye of Truth and hear
his voice listening to us.
Listen to what the Source says,
saying to you
think more of what you must do
and go beyond to your fullest potential
of enjoying Life
with your attitude.

The Fires 2020

Game of Thrones, Bernie Sanders, Donald Trump,
Black Lives Matter, Mauna Kea telescope,
Obama/Biden memes

Floating island made of trash, Epstein, Tiger King,
Coronavirus, Quarantine, neo-Nazis

Ryan started the fire!
It was always burnin' since the world was turnin'
Ryan started the fire!
It was always burnin' since the world was turnin'

earthquakes, hurricanes, California up in flames,
kids in cages, Disney remakes, Dumbledore is gay

Kim Jong-un, marijuana, Middle East, Hong Kong,
Hamilton, Putin, Brexit, and the Bataclan

Ryan started the fire!
It was always burnin' since the world was turnin'
Ryan started the fire!
It was always burnin' since the world was turnin'

Carrie Fischer, Banksy, UFOs, school shootings,
Dakota Access Pipeline, police brutality

transgender internet, Netflix, Dragon X,
9/11, Amazon prime, climate change, Harambe

Ryan started the fire!
It was always burnin' since the world was turnin'
Ryan started the fire!
It was always burnin' since the world was turnin'

※

Moaning about the loss of home values,
staring into the screens.
To us, many of those values were a fairytale,
taught with words but not actions.
Repetitious motions of a finger
relay complacent, compliant cruelty,
showing the world hypocrisy
of words that never line up with action
from our absorbent seats.
You're not being yourself
when you're being a brainwashed
right-wing version of a person,
when you're being a self-righteous
left-wing version of a person.
When the evidence is presented,
your filter is too strongly steeped
to see beyond immediate argument
to the realm where thought pervades,
shouting louder and longer lies to each other
given your soft weapons to fling with rage
then walk away and cry
about the absence of discourse
keeping to your unmanageable prejudice
and in hatred blaming others for your fear
without education of the cause.
A loner has more reason than ever to recluse,
a listener bombarded by talk
and he sees
they're filling their snowballs with rocks,
gone past disagreement
to malicious war,
but it's all the pre-paid stories
and rotating pictures
convincing you to sneer at others
doing exactly as you do,

while gorging secretly
are the program-shifters.
Each generation has a loss of values.
Each generation has reclaiming.
Each generation has unwilling complacency
and the search for knowledge,
willful ignorance
and a need to be free
beyond ourselves.
A man is sitting
as they yell and fling rocks,
in meditation he sees they are all free
and trapped in their memory.
But, he must climb the mountain
to be at the peak,
not amidst their distracted reek.
The greyed green air of ceaseless gas
shifting around in the valley
will settle, the man will come down to their aftermath,
and they will be ripped and torn
and it will take long years
for the air to be clear
before the one tribe picks itself up
gathering each other to embrace with no distinction
the differences which were not there
and which they can no longer see
and carry each other, walking, supported
in a great migration to a sunny, merry beach.

Stop complaining about the loss of values,
stop calling it values and start calling it value
and you'll see it everywhere, and in everyone.

※

The midnight wakefulness
of shattered self-anger
of self-conscious delaying, of decay, of unhappiness
then dreams to wake us, yelling but stifled, haunting
of egotistic cruelty which you portray
the sonnets are pain to a man devoured
he can barely read each letter
those who help are irritated
as the help doesn't truly fit
and whether on an unsatisfactory bicycle
or a falling down horse
in the rain, it is catastrophe
to be aided by the self-concerned grasping
the disasters of a fire travelling spell
which smokes and lets one, but not you, through
to a dimension in safety
as you are chased by those
who attack and release responsibility
of their offense
as they cry at your self-defense
and you give another a talisman to escape
and they're thankful, and they'll
find their own harbor
and at last, you step out to the smoky red dawn
and are caught by autumn's grip

but the hawk in the morning wakes us up slow

A mark of the sea upon his brow…

The song of the kiss of the blessed blend rang
and he called to the heavens in his loudest howl
"Hear me! I am in need of sight!"
and he heard, You have it.
from a smiling voice,
You are not a king. You are a god.
"Then why do I feel such sadness?"
That is a god's portion.
But, do not fret. Do not fear.
You will have a happy life
if you release your worry.

※

Dancing in the desert
imagining the drums
and return home
the beat is wrecking
and I will live my dream